Soul Sisters

Shine as brightly as you were meant to shine

By Marion Graham

Copyright 2010 by Soul Success Ltd.
Published by Soul Success Ltd.

★

CONTENTS

★

PREFACE

16th April 2007 the day the book was born!!
This book aims to empower women and enlighten men.

Soul Sisters is a book of new beginnings, a book that encourages women to step into their personal power and strengthen who they are. However, this is also a book for men. A book that allows men to better understand the women that they work and live with, leading to a degree of insight and understanding that allows relationships to progress and develop while both sexes exist in harmony.

This book has been a long time coming and at one point was almost lost to the idea that "The Rules of Coaching" should be the topic of my first book. However the universe had a different plan for me and over a 12 month period I was presented with life experiences that pulled my thoughts back to the wonderful women of the world who often leave little or no time for themselves as individuals.

Our women come with many labels attached, daughter, sister, mother, wife, aunt, friend, lover as well as labels linked to our paid employment. Over the coming chapters we will explore the roles that women embrace and the price that we can pay for losing ourselves to the labels.

Every role we play is important but equally important is taking the time to be ourselves and enjoy activities, pastimes and pursuits that are solely for our benefit. Moments of relaxation and reflection are the key to growth, development and balance. Woman must learn to build in time to recharge and replenish the energy that they so freely give to others and to do so without feeling guilty. The men of our world are much better at understanding the need to have time out for recreation and the benefit of placing importance on free time. We have much to learn from men and we can do so without compromising our own gender.

Our journey together will be interactive and you will be invited to take time- out along the way to reflect on past experience and celebrate past successes. The book is your learning partner as you plan the next stage into the unknown and you are invited to visualise the future in positive and exciting ways to give you the strongest chance to live life to the full.

★

INTRODUCTION

It is my firm belief that women can achieve more if they work together and support and encourage each other leaving behind the need to judge and measure who is smartest, richest, slimmest or most attractive. This book takes us on our journey of empowerment and can be read by our partners in life, be they male or female, life partners or business partners, they can choose to observe our journey or participate on their own wonderful adventure at the same time. The choice is yours.

I have had many strong positive role models in my life and have friends that belong to several different generations. When I decided to write my book I was encouraged by both male and female friends to let my mind flow freely and trust my intuition to choose the topic.

Strange as it seems I knew I had to write my book but dithered between business coaching, training & development, personal coaching and the topic that won the day was indeed Soul Sisters, a book that contained my thoughts and ideas on what makes our life journey less challenging and more exciting.

I was born the youngest of 3 children; my sister Jan who was 11 years older, and my brother Tom who was 9 years older I was the baby. I enjoyed the privileges that this place in the family brings, butting into conversations and dancing in the middle of the room waiting for applause and adoration. I thrived on the extra attention and the praise; it gave me the high self esteem and the confidence to do what I do now.

My mother Ruby was, and still is, a lovely kind caring wee woman who worked hard and could turn her hand to anything, knitting, sewing, baking, decorating and nursing. She endeavoured to keep my feet on the ground by praising when she felt it was due but also pushing me to always do a little more than I would have on my own. In her opinion there was no room for time wasting and a job had to be given your best shot every time. As I grew up and my brother moved down south and my sister moved up north my mother used to say "Where would I be without my baby" I often thought she could have been away sailing round the world on a luxury cruise but the thought of such extravagance never crossed her mind! So I was blessed with loving supportive parents.

All through my life I have focused on the positive and was raised by a father who had indeed arrived in this world before his time. Bert Gourlay, born 1920, was interested in books that helped you increase your height, astrology charts, working out formulas for his "bookies lines" for his 50 pence bets on the horses, history, philosophy and current affairs. He was my best coach ever, my encourager and my friend. He never hesitated to listen to my opinion from the moment I could talk, this was very early and I've never really stopped! Right up until the day he passed away he always recognised me as a strong independent young woman with an opinion that was worth listening to and this made me feel very valuable indeed. No other form of encouragement is quite as powerful.

Who we are starts with the nurturing that we receive as children but if we were not so fortunate to feel cherished we have to learn to love ourselves and start now. Loving and respecting yourself by taking the time to know yourself, know your strengths, know your standards and live a life where you do what you do with pleasure and pride. You are unique you are special you are a gift to the world and have lots to offer. Only by taking time for you will you know what you are capable of. You are most definitely capable of more than you have ever imagined. Now isn't that an exciting prospect?

- This book is aimed at Women who want to invest in themselves. It is an inward bound rather than an outward bound experience and it encourages women to feel beautiful inside and beautiful outside and take up their rightful place in the world. All the women and men that read this book are different, all with their own story and their own unique skill set. I want us to end the book feeling we have a place at any table we choose to sit at. I want us to say "I am good enough as I am".

- The book is about making connections for life & business. It is a chance to network, getting out there and making the effort to know other women and men. There will be businesses that complement yours and women you can learn from. Strength comes from people able to share, people who have a prosperity mindset.

- I want you to have a learning experience that is uplifting, enlightening and enjoyable. I would like you to end the book with a positive attitude, focused on success.

- You are all wonderful women with the capacity for greatness.

- The questions that are asked today will be the triggers for personal change. The answers are important but not always immediate.

REFLECTION SECTION

Each chapter ends on a reflection section to encourage you to choose to develop a new habit and also to value the act of self giving, taking time to think about your life journey and plan of action.

What do I want you to get from this reflection?

I would like you to get personal growth, vision, focus, confidence, purpose, motivation and a sense of self. I would like you to consider who you would like to be, where would you like to be and what you would like to do? Exciting thoughts that you may not have fully explored yet.... Well let the journey begin.

Maximise your moment free your spirit and step into the light. These reflections are about believing and achieving, celebrating success, strengthening women and encouraging you to step into your personal power. Often we spend our time running faster than the rest of the world the time we take in reflection is our time to drop down a gear and enjoy the slower pace.

Reflection Time

As we begin this journey together take the time to reflect on the questions below and allow the answers to come and write them down. Be honest with yourself as this is the secret to your success.

- Who are my encouragers in life right now?
- Who are my friends?
- What do I get from each of them and what do I give?
- How do I feel about my place in my birth family?
- What positive memories do I have of my parents?
- What was I like as a child?
- Who was my best coach as I was being raised?

Bottom Line

Great you have joined me.

Let's step out on a journey of self awareness. These questions will kick start a habit of self reflection. Enjoy! Make them our choices, we can decide what we have and what we do. We can, perhaps for the first time, choose to do what makes our heart sing.

★

CENTRED ON SUCCESS

As they say in Scotland "Ah cannae wait", indicating excitement, joy and anticipation for something great! That's how I feel about the amazing chance we have to reshape and remould the lives we are living. Perhaps we need to shave away things that no longer serve us well or we need to embrace the new and exciting, living for the present and going for it.

Soul Sisters is a short and sweet development opening for those with limited time. For those of us old enough to remember getting a pay packet at the end of the working week, the deductions and tax and national insurance were of no consequence all we wanted to see was what was left on the bottom line, the money left for us to use to enjoy life to the full. Chances are we were young and carefree then so let's recreate that feeling one more time and with gusto! Yes this is a chance to see the bottom line near the top! Really that's what we all want isn't it?

This book begins your journey and the revelations will amaze you. We know from the seminars delivered that the graduates have experienced life changing moments, all of which they can take total credit for. Our ladies have gone on to get the jobs they wanted, overcome fears, set up businesses, increased profits, rented allotments and taken time to relax.

"Soul Sisters" is a programme for women who truly want to be successful. The book is an introduction to and preparation for the programme, it aims to refresh and reinforce all that is positive and special about you.

This book, like the programme should help you feel

- Confident
- Motivated
- Unique
- Creative
- Valuable
- Happy
- Successful

As we journey I urge you to take time to complete the Reflection at the end of the Sections, note what I said "TAKE TIME". No- one ever gives us time on a plate, we have to take and make time for ourselves. For those in a hurry who like to recap I have added a Bottom Line.

CONFIDENCE

When asked what they would like more of most women on my courses say; confidence. What makes us feel confident?

Confidence starts from within. The biggest favour we do ourselves is by talking ourselves up and not down, by imagining that we look the part, sound the part and are equal to others in the room, no better, no less just on the same level as the other human beings we meet.

When I work with individuals on increasing confidence I am constantly repeating "you must feel that you have a place at any table." During my 7 years working with Prince Charles' Charity, The Prince's Trust, I met with people from every conceivable background, celebrities, business gurus, royalty and young people, some with challenging pasts. The one thing that made my job easier was that I was happy to be who I was and find out who they were regardless of the label that had been attached to them. Looking well groomed without a doubt makes us more confident, spending time selecting what you wear and scrubbing up for each occasion. However putting your best self forward means choosing your attitude for the day as well as your outfit. We can choose to get out there and expect the best; every day can be an adventure but that adventure, excitement and positive expectation starts in our own head and has to be reinforced and recreated each and every day. The first step to a confident you is to see yourself there. See yourself being the sort of woman who has a place at any table. Visualise others clambering to get a seat next to you because you are so great to be with, imagine how good that feels.

One of the affirmations that works best for me when I push myself out of my comfort zone is to tell myself "I am enough just as I am " over and over again!!

REFLECTION SECTION

on Confidence

- List 7 things that make you feel good about who you are?

1.

2.

3.

4.

5.

6.

7.

- List the behaviours that you associate with confidence and confident people?

- Can you begin to adopt this style of behaviour?

- When?

The Bottom Line - Confidence

Now all that remains is to start work on your own belief system and feed your subconscious mind all those positive words and thoughts about being a popular choice for any guest list. Increase your confidence now!

MOTIVATION

Motivated individuals have a sense of purpose and know where they are going and what they want out of life. We are all motivated by different things. People can be motivated by money and the bigger the financial gain the harder they try. Others are motivated by personal pride, by what others think of them, others by image, fame, family or the thought of freedom. No one can motivate you, they can point out the benefits of being fully motivated and up for it but you are the one that has to take the action.

When you are motivated you are ready to take on the world and feel that you can achieve anything. Choosing the company of people who are upbeat and go getters does help us feel that we can push harder and achieve more. Sitting side by side with a moaner and groaner can grind you down and their lack of purpose and miserable attitude makes us feel that it's all an up hill struggle. That is why programmes and courses that bring together people with higher energies and a desire to be motivated and succeed are a perfect place to step yourself forward with purpose, motivated and ready to get what you want from life.

It is almost as if we have to have permission to be positive and that we don't want to appear too driven in case people get the wrong idea. The time to be motivated is now before we turn into a nation of losers afraid to reach our potential and struggling with mediocrity. Don't settle for average or below. Decide on what you want and fire yourself up to get it.

Sharing your vision and allowing others to enhance the picture and refine your goal can clearly effect your motivation; that's why having a personal coach means you achieve more. Your coach takes no action, nor do they decide when and how you will move forward, but they do rekindle the sparks that fan the flames that ignites the belief that "you can."

REFLECTION SECTION

on Motivation

- So list the 7 things that motivate you?

1.

2.

3.

4.

5.

6.

7.

- What is your focus, what drives you?

- Are you ready to step up to the mark, set your sights and take the action to get the results that you want and deserve?

- When?

The Bottom Line - Motivation

All that remains now is for you to choose the action that you take and charge yourself up, fully motivated and with your sights clearly set on getting what you want and what you deserve in life, love and work.

BEING UNIQUE

We are all unique, we are all different. We all have unique abilities and we all have talents and strengths that set us apart from the crowd. The challenge is for us to celebrate our differences. We often sabotage who we are by being under confident. We pussy foot around until we blend rather than shine. By shining I mean being who we are, being who we were meant to be and loving that person just as they are. We admire other people's qualities and strengths but when did you last congratulate yourself for what you do well?

When we have a real unique ability we tend to think that every one shines in this area, if we find something easy we never credit ourselves with being extra talented to achieve what we are achieving but devalue our skill by thinking that it is not our talent that makes this a task quickly completed but the simplicity of the task.

For example you may be a great organiser and as soon as there is an event or occasion that requires planning you have lists, phone numbers, dates to achieve things by and much, much more. By the time you have achieved this everyone else has just got to the stage that they agreed that the event is a good idea. You however have planned it from start to finish in your head! This is a skill, this is a unique ability. You are different, you have different qualities and you are blessed to be this way.

How do we rate what we do well and how do we maximise our moment in relation to our skill set? We may have to engage the help of people who know us well to allow them to confirm what sets us apart from the crowd in the most positive way. This is an exercise that you may squirm at as we don't take praise positively and are often imagining that there is an ulterior motive for kind words. Stop, stop, stop!! Listen, assess, acknowledge and enjoy the chance to have others say it like it is and learn the qualities that you should market, develop and be proud of.

REFLECTION SECTION
on Being Unique

- List the 7 skills/qualities that set you apart from the crowd?

1.

2.

3.

4.

5.

6.

7.

- Ask 4 other people who know you to list the top skills or qualities that set you apart from the crowd. Select these individuals from your world of work, family and friends.

- List your top qualities that appear most often

The Bottom Line - Being Unique
Being different is good. It means we can complement rather than compete in teams and in personal relationships. Take time to pat yourself on the back and be grateful that we are all individual.

CREATIVE

Most people tell me that they are not creative, but what makes them think that?

People are afraid to think of themselves as creative because it means you have to come up with new and different ways of doing things and thinking about things. It means you will be singled out from the crowd again and there will be an expectation that you are able to problem solve and come up with creative solutions.

If we are confident we are happy to suggest ideas and put our views and opinions forward because guess what? We understand that we won't always get it spot on, get it right or solve the problems all the time but we have a go and sometimes, just sometimes we crack it!

So creativity is the ability to start with nothing and plan or make something. It is the ability to shape, to mould and to work towards an end result. There are endless possibilities when we begin to create because it is about imagining how things could be; it is not about the exact science of getting it right first time every time. We all have the ability to imagine but as we reach adulthood we can detach and distance ourselves from imagining how things might be. We see imagining or daydreaming as time wasting in adults. Strange because man or boy, woman or girl creativity starts with imaginative thought.

Possibilities, choices, a dream of how things could be, should be, would be and finally how things are going to be. Think of the saying "You can't solve a problem with the mind that created it." Well thank goodness for that because now we have the chance to recreate, change and manage our issues and our world in a more upbeat and exciting way by seeing the best possible solutions and creating the future that we wish for ourselves and others.

REFLECTION SECTION
on Creativity

- List the 7 benefits that you imagine come from being creative?

1.

2.

3.

4.

5.

6.

7.

- What is creativity?

- Who do you know that you think is creative?

- What do you think makes them creative?

- How do you imagine you could become more creative?

The Bottom Line - Creativity
Start imagining more; give yourself permission to dream brilliant positive thoughts. Have the experience of how things might be and create several different paths, plans or outcomes.

VALUABLE

I start by saying that everyone has a value and the more you contribute the more valuable you become, but what you have to realise is that as well as giving to others you have to give to yourself.

We touch on so many lives that it is almost impossible to imagine the impact that we make throughout our years. The movie "It's a Wonderful Life" encapsulates the idea of one person's value and worth in the most powerful way.

The movies focus, George Baillie, feels he has under achieved because he parked his dreams of travel and excitement and stayed in his home town; he now faces financial ruin and wishes himself dead. In so doing his guardian angel is sent down to create the world without George Baillie. We see the people in Bedford Falls and how they have underachieved and gone off track because he did not live and therefore could not touch their lives.

We are all George Baillie, valuable, making a difference not only to our nearest and dearest but to the person that you wave to in the morning at the train station, or to the child that you said was the best cyclist in the school. Our words and actions have the ripple effect of going on and on.

The lesson to be learned is to allow yourself time out and to value who you are by only agreeing to do what you can and knowing when to say no because you need to do something for you and achieve something for you that increases your self worth and self belief. Take time to feel how valuable you are.

REFLECTION SECTION
on Valuable

What value do we place on our life, our contribution and our relationships with friends and family?

- What do we value?

- Who do we value?

- How much do we value ourselves?

- What makes us a valuable asset to our community?

- What makes you personally feel valuable?

- Is it important to value ourselves?

The Bottom Line - Valuable
People value individuals who value themselves. Acknowledge the difference that we all make to others through the time, energy, passion, love and commitment that we freely give. Understand the value that comes from theses priceless gifts.

HAPPY

Someone once said we are about as happy as we make our minds up to be; now there is more than a grain of truth in that!

My friend Margaret McCathie is a Laughter Therapist and is in no doubt that we are responsible for our own joy.........but not for anyone else's joy.

A few years back I was arranging a special birthday party for my lovely husband and, being human, was feeling the stress of it all. I met up with Margaret and she clearly could see that the organising and planning was taking its toll. She asked me several questions, "Have you booked a venue?" Yes it was booked and paid for. "Have you booked music for the night?" Yes I replied. "Have you arranged food for the guests", yes I had. "Will there be refreshments?" She asked, there sure will I replied! Then what's the worry was Margaret's take on all this? Clearly she stated, you have taken all the basic needs into consideration and all that remains is for your guests to come along and bring their own joy with them and the night will be complete.

Sounds simple doesn't it? Yet we all fall into the trap of considering other people's happiness before our own on occasions and this means we sell ourselves short. The more joyful we are the more joy we bring to others and the more we concentrate on the joy of the moment the better life gets.

We have to look for our happiness and decide what makes us feel good. We can have a good day every day by taking pleasure in small things and allowing our hearts to sing when we see and experience others joy. I am uplifted by watching happy people and happy occasions. We can steep ourselves in the dull and the dark and the boring because there is so much of it out there. Break free smile, and see what happens.....people smile back.

REFLECTION SECTION
on Happiness

- Who makes you happy?

- What makes you happy?

- Are you responsible for others happiness?

- How can you increase or decrease the amount of joy you feel?

- How often do we consider our own happiness?

The Bottom Line - Happiness
You are responsible for your own joy and happiness. Frightening or freeing ....you decide!! What may make it a little easier is you are not responsible for anyone else's joy; they have to take ownership too!!

SUCCESS

Success will be different things to different people.

For me success starts from within and if my personal relationship with myself is good then I have the beginnings of success. The reason my company is called "Soul Success" is to emphasis how important your relationship with you is. People invest no time in reflection, relaxation, recuperation and then they wonder why they are not succeeding. You wouldn't work an animal without resting it so why treat yourself less than you would a working beast.

We incorrectly link pressure and stress with success and think that those who run fastest for longest are successful, are hamsters on a wheel successful? Think about train journeys that you take that may be around an hour when people are commuting to work. Count the number of people who get the mobile out and make calls... now ask yourself how many were necessary and how many were made to endorse the always busy, always on the phone, always pushed to the limit stressed out/ successful business executive. Anxiety pushes us to always keep busy. One great speaker said I'm not busy, I'm successful......... food for thought in the manic world we live in.

When I was working in Edinburgh recently I took time out to go to the "Cornerstone Café" linked to St John's Church on Lothian Road to relax and revive before my next coaching session and before I had coffee I browsed in the book shop next door where I picked up this little poem titled "Success". Real words of wisdom copied opposite!

Success is speaking words of praise
In cheering other people's ways
In doing just the best you can
With every task and every plan
It's silence when your speech would hurt
Politeness when your neighbour's curt
It's deafness when the scandal flows
And sympathy with others woes
It's loyalty when duty calls
It's courage when disaster falls
It's found in laughter and in song
It's in the silent time of prayer
In happiness and in despair
In all of life and nothing less
We find the thing we call success

REFLECTION SECTION
on Success

- Who do you admire and rate as a successful individual?

- What are their qualities?

- What is true success?

- What is success for you?

The Bottom Line - Success
Soul success is being grounded, true to you and having balance in all that you do. Don't be fooled into thinking that running about taking and making phone calls and working all hours makes you a success it doesn't it makes you tired.

Let's promise ourselves the best year yet and have a lot more fun and less frantic worry and challenge. I am so sure that you will move on rapidly after each reflection that I am already planning the follow up book............ "Soul Sisters Stories" which will be your book dedicated to your success and your achievements following your passage from frantic to free!!

★

LETTING GO

I believe we have all carried an invisible rucksack on our back filled with all our issues, challenges and problems past and present. The thing about this rucksack is that it is like a bottomless pit capable of harbouring infinite worry and hardship.

Every worry is like a lead weight and the more we store the more we are weighed down. Have a think about the concerns, challenges and problems that are part of your past that you carry with you to this day. Why are you carrying them? Are they helpful? I'm not suggesting that you suppress them rather that you deal with them by deciding what you can do to improve the situation and letting go what can't be changed. The experience of letting go can be painful but when you are ready to let go, and choose to, the feeling that ultimately remains is one of relief. You can once again begin to smile, relax and enjoy life.

Talk the challenges out of your mind and in so doing out of your system then move on! I am not suggesting this is easy but it is necessary for good mental health. Let's leave behind any issues or challenges that we have, be it with us or others. This in turn opens our mind and allows us to be solution orientated in the way we think. Take time, listen to your heart and mind, leave behind your luggage of life and move on with a lighter spirit.

It's often acceptable to moan, wail, whine and churn over what's missing in our lives and who sold us short. Every single time we talk about the injustice of a situation, a person, an establishment or a hurt, our energy levels fall and we feed the worry monster that holds permanent residence in the penthouse suite of our mind. Think about the amount of time you give over to worry and then think of the amount of time you give over to fun and creative, imaginative thinking. We work with an 80/20 rule in most things in life. If 80% of the time is in state of worry with 20% given to fun you won't have much to smile about and laughter will be an all too fleeting pleasure. Choose change. Choose to let go. Choose 80% of the time to be positive focused and in "can do" mode. Choose to be light and bright and choose it now! Choose fun!

Why do we hold negative emotion? Who is really affected or hurt by our inability to let go? We are the ones that suffer from the grudges that we hold against others. The planning of vendettas in our mind and churning over wrong doings causes our positivity to decrease. We are the ones who suffer the pain, the shame and the energy dip. We cause ourselves to feel uncomfortable due to the worry we evoke. Dis-ease in our minds leads to disease in the body. Dis-ease is exactly what it implies; it is a state of mind or body in which we feel ill at ease and uncomfortable with ourselves. This discomfort or dis-ease of our mind and spirit leads to the silent killer of the 21st century; STRESS! Letting go of negative emotion decreases stress and allows us to be at ease.

As adults we seem to think we only gain our pass into the "grown up land" if we can bring a worry to the table. But "grown up land" doesn't have to be "groan up" land! Does worry make you a better friend, parent, lover or does it makes you miserable? I remember being at a personal development seminar where people had to share their journey of life from childhood to adulthood. I was one of the last to share and as each delegate took to the floor the theme seemed to be doom, gloom, heartache and challenge. Was the purpose to make them appear more successful due to the unhappiness and imbalance that they had experienced, was it to get the Oscar for the most heart wrenching story? Or was it that we exaggerate and recall misery because it is the accepted norm in society? More accepted than talking about excitement, pleasure and joy? I almost felt I would have to invent a worry or challenge to be part of the gang. I am sure many have had similar "working class" upbringings like my own, it's all about the memories we choose to hold and the ones we let go. Our national press seems to glorify the depressing and the depressed and dismiss the happy and the successful as unsubstantial cheese. Well as one of my most positive friends Susan would say give me cheese any day I love cheese!

Now I am not suggesting for a minute that we dismiss all concerns and issues that are part of reality, far from it. Find a friend, ask them if they are free to listen and have a good old session where you talk through your cares and woes then choose to let go. This friend has to be a very special type I call these friends my Sunshine& Showers friends because they are tough enough to offer a shoulder to cry on, they don't blab to the world and they can lift your spirits by throwing some humour even on the most difficult worry. My "pal fae school" Dorothy knows within 30 seconds of talking to me if I have a worry niggling at the back of my mind.........this is both wonderful and infuriating at the same time. We may feel sophisticated enough to mask negative emotion but it seems not!! Still we should be thankful to friends who see through our masks and feel blessed by their love and concern for us.

Seeking approval is another area where we tend to have a DESPERATE need to let go. Why should we worry about what people think of us if we are living our lives doing no harm and being considerate and careful about other people's feelings? I often tell my friends and clients that we are not answerable to others nor do we need their permission to take a certain action or make a specific choice. We are the masters of our destiny, we sail the ship, we choose the route, we decide on the destination. Or is that the problem; have we allowed others to influence us into travelling a path of their choosing and stopping when it suits them. If that is the case you have a choice you CAN change and move on......... prepare to ruffle a few feathers, a small price to pay for freedom and independence.

Freedom means being true to you. If there was a movie made of your life and you were in control you would be the star of the show, you would be the director, you would write the script, you would choose your leading lady or man and you would audition the extras that you felt made the best possible movie. You would thank the others who auditioned but were unsuitable and in the nicest possible way you would wish them luck and bid them farewell. We are talking about personal power. Personal power often frightens people. Why? Well, if YOU take full responsibility for you there is no one to blame if things go pear shaped, often no one to chastise, no one to point the finger at , the responsibility for your success is entirely down to you. The truth is this is always the case anyway even if you choose to blame others!

Some people never choose to let go choosing nasty over nice, pain over pleasure, stress over relaxation and always looking to blame others. Happiness will always elude them because they are not happy with themselves. They value money, possession, status and titles that inflate their worth. They consider no one, and yet their belief is that they should be first on everyone's "Christmas card list" and be given consideration and priority over the rest of the world. Who makes them this way? We do, friends, family, employees dancing to the bully's tune and afraid to be who we are and say no.

We have to hold our hands up to self sabotage, moments when we compromise who we are and what we want. We give our power to someone else with the false belief that they know best. No one knows you better than you know yourself. No one will travel the journey of life with you from start to finish every step of the way. Start listening to your inner voice the positive, pleasant one who doles out praise and accolade not criticism and negative nagging.

We are different from men, we do things our way; we should make no apology for being unique. Let go of the need to criticise, look for the best in others, always offering positive feedback for change or praise for getting it right. Same sex sabotage is common in female groups. Women can be critical of other women whether it is jealousy, insecurity, fear, it is something to let go of if we want to take centre stage for success and reach our potential. Women need to champion other women.

To appreciate how unhelpful it is to hold onto things. We end this chapter and begin our next stage of change by lightening our load. This is our emotional clear out!

Begin to let go and promise yourself to look on these reflection sections as your "out to play time". Promise to bring your whole self into this reflection and development session armed with the knowledge that there are no fairies to wave magic wands and do our work as we take reflection time BUT there is nothing that won't wait and NOTHING that is more important than you! So we begin by reprogramming our belief systems allowing our mind to be de-cluttered.

Society is suffering from "affluenza" a phrase coined by the author Oliver James in his book of the same title. Recent decades brought extra cash and allowed us to buy more possession. We could all probably have a massive clear out, give away half of what we own, and never miss what we had given away. We've entered an age of constant communication where we are viewing and measuring what others have and do. With social networking, mobile phones, mini laptops and Blackberry type devices encouraging us to sneak a peek into other people's business; we are leaving ourselves less time to tend to our own business. This is the time to get reconnected with YOUR business and shift what no longer serves you well.

LET GO OF YOUR LUGGAGE OF LIFE

- Let go of the past. We can't change it and there is no bonus in carrying a lifetime of worries and negative comments with us!
- Clear the clutter. Think of your mind as a wardrobe and your thoughts like the clothes that you no longer need, perhaps you have out grown them, or they no longer suit you.
- Forgive and move on.

  A grudge hurts you more than anyone else.
- Drop the grudge and feel the relief instead of the pain.
- Don't pick the worry or grudge up again. Break the cycle!
- Change stumbling blocks to stepping stones.
- See the possibilities not the problems.
- Release the pressure, whoever or whatever puts you under pressure let it go.
- Make the time to write down the luggage of life.
- Then release, forgive and move on.
- Don't discuss challenges continually
- Don't share negative thoughts with everyone.
- Write them down and pledge to let go.
- Repeat often!
- Destroy the list of luggage of life. Let this symbolic gesture clear worry leaving space for the magic of life.
- This is the start of a process, the first step to being in the moment and living for now.
- Begin your journey from where you are now far removed from your past.
- Decide where you would like to be and take the first step.

REFLECTION SECTION
on Letting Go

Take time to list your luggage of life

- What from your past was holding you back?

- Who from your past was holding you back?

- What thoughts are no longer serving you well?

- What are your fears?

- Could you let all of this go?

- Are you ready to let it go?

- Will you let it go now?

The Bottom Line - Letting Go

Decide how you mark the releasing of that which is holding you back. Shred it, rip it into small pieces or burn it in the fire. Heck! Dance naked over the still glowing embers if it floats your boat. Most importantly make it permanent and invest your energy in the new and exciting.

Let go of it all. The man who stole your parking space this morning, your brother who never phones, your sister who never visits your mother, your son who leaves towels on the bathroom floor, the boss who never communicates, the colleague who is always moaning; wave good-bye with a secret smile.

★

WHAT DO WOMEN WANT

A question significant enough to inspire a Mel Gibson movie! So...

What do women want?

- ★ Do we know what we want?
- ★ Do we take the time to consider what is best for us or do we constantly flit from pillar to post in an attempt to please everyone?
- ★ Are women afraid to say "This is what I want"? Why?
- ★ Or, do woman say what they want?
- ★ How do they say it?
- ★ Do they say it confidently, apologetically, aggressively, assertively, quietly or loudly?
- ★ Do women feel they are entitled to get what they want?
- ★ Do they feel there is a price to pay?
- ★ Should there be a price to pay for stating/getting what you want?

Lots of questions, requiring lots of answer. Women are great at asking questions but are we great at answering them? See there's me at it again! Often when life goes out of balance we look at who is to blame. I'd like to ask you now to stand alone, take responsibility for your life, and apportion no blame. That's right, none at all, not even to yourself.

The most important thing to do when there is less balance in our life is to examine the key areas that contribute to balance; take a snapshot of our life. We can do this by scoring each of the key areas on a scale of 1 to 10, the higher the score the better we feel things are in this area, the lower the score the more challenges we have in that area. The areas of our life that require improvement in order to restore balance become immediately clear and apparent. This scoring system highlights where you choose to focus and allows you to check your self-satisfaction in each area. The main aim is to have life in balance and if one section is a 10/10 and one a 2/10 it will be a pretty bumpy ride!

The tool we use to measure and calculate where we are in our journey is called "The Circle of Life." "The Circle of Life" has real visual impact and may be the catalyst required to spur you on towards effective goal setting, encouraging you to stay on track by verbalising and visualising the goals you have committed to paper. This exercise looks at the value you place in each section of your circle of life and exposes your current life balance in a safe environment. This allows you to take action of your own and have a clearer vision of the direction for your future.

We concentrate on 8 key areas choosing the most popular that affect our life balance and harmony. Choose 8 from the list below

- Family
- Friends
- Personal relationship
- Health
- Fitness
- Career
- Personal Development
- Education
- Finance
- Spirituality
- Recreation

Start with real honesty and mark each area a score. When you have finished connect each area in a join the dots session one to the other. Now look at the shape you have, not many people have a circle so before you start to panic remember, whatever the shape it is YOURS and it provides you with a starting point for your journey towards balance. Let's look at each area in more depth and decide on how we score. Complete the Circle of Life on the next page.

Circle of Life of...
Date....................

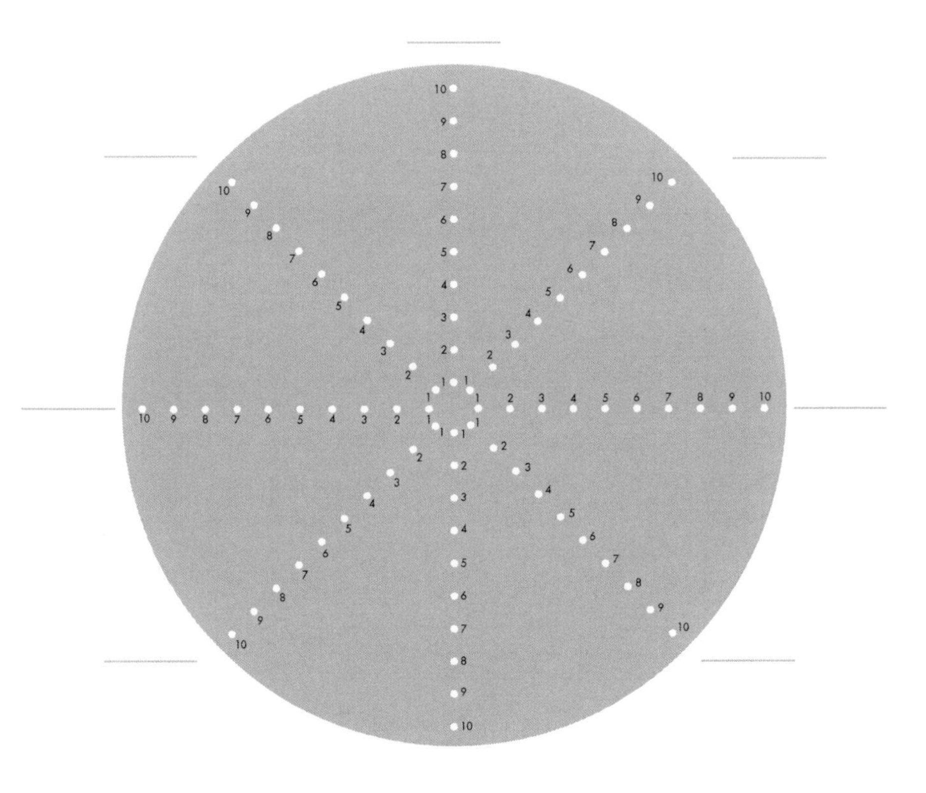

Example

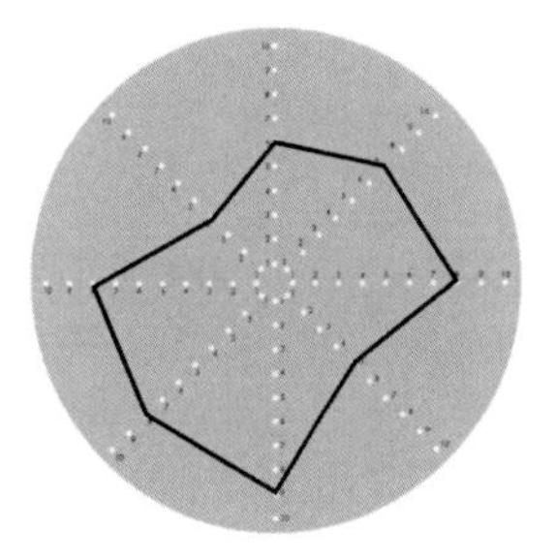

We should take 30 minutes quiet time to select the areas that we will review and honestly and truthfully reflect on how life is at present.

Often we are so busy running that we don't consider how our life is shaping up. We are the masters of our destiny, the energy and force behind our progress yet we often float rather than steer our own ship. They say that if you fail to prepare then you should prepare to fail. We want to be fully prepared to sail on course taking the most scenic route and enjoying any stops that we choose to make along the way. Life is about embracing and enjoying as well as working and achieving.

This short exercise allows you to "Maximise your Moment" by putting pen to paper and planning your next course in the journey of life. Those who take time to look at where they are and what is happening to them and those around them are the ones who achieve the most, and yet we have to be cajoled into investing in ourselves in this way. I urge you to invest now in you and become one of the special few who have vision and a map for the next stage. If you have a life map in place, excellent, but it is also necessary to go with the flow. You may have a map for the next stage in life however life does not always go to plan, it's ok to change course and direction at any moment, the only person who decides on this is you. Let's look at our areas of importance.

FAMILY

Family can be split into immediate family and extended family before we consider how much time, effort and energy goes into it. Is there one person in particular that demands time and leaves you struggling to see anyone else or is there someone who deserves more of your time but who says little and gets little? Family can uplift us or drain us but it is important that we choose to give time without being pressurised by guilt. We should give our time, money and talents to our family willingly. Any gift that is given willingly is twice as precious to the receiver. I tend to remember most those who have given so much to me and who have shaped me and made me who I am today. I choose to give them my time and energy and aim to do this willingly. I am aware we are mere grains of sand on the beach of time so family are extremely important to me especially the elders of the tribe!

As well as giving, it is vital to receive support and help from family. If we don't ask when we need our family to be there for us we deny them the privilege of providing for us. We all love the feeling of being able to love, nurture, care and provide for, it is food for our soul and strengthens our bonds. Sometimes you must ask in order to receive, never assume someone knows that you need them, even your nearest and dearest. This two way street can be busy but manageable if we are open and honest about what we can give and what we would like to receive. Say it like it is and measure the balance when you are open and honest and happy about exchanging energy and talents. Families can be our greatest source of balance and love if we get it right.

It is never too late to change the way we view our family. Bridges can be built with a phone call, letter, visit or a quick text. We all need to know our place is safe and secure in our family unit and we can all be the carer and the cared for. Take time to decide on how you would like it to be, after you have honestly looked at how it is presently. Taking all this into account is a major task as you decide how your family, who can be the source of both huge joy and huge frustration, affect your life balance. Are your family ties too tight, too slack or completely cut off and how does this affect you when you are mixing, working and socialising with the rest of the world? It serves us well to look to these first and lasting relationships when making new ones.

FRIENDS

Friends are so important in our lives; they fill many of our emotional needs taking the pressure off our families and life partners. Clichéd as it might be, friends truly are the family we choose for ourselves and can provide great emotional support. As siblings grow up they often grow apart. Family growing apart can happen for a variety of reasons linked to location and what you have in common. Friends can be chosen because they have shared interests, they live near by, they are the same age or are at the same stage or because they are totally different!! The secret to balance with friends for me is choice and not need; it's the desire to share experiences and occasions with wonderful people who make us happy.

Like family, we want friends in our lives who will be there for us when the going gets tough, people who are honest, but not unnecessarily harsh, with us, and people who are loyal and supportive through the showers as well as the sunshine. To maintain great friendships this arrangement must be reciprocal. So how do you score the balance between you and your friends? Are things tickety boo or is there more need than want, more misery than magic? Are your friends' high maintenance or high quality? Or is quantity your concern?

Do you need more friends in life? Have you a good mix of personalities or do you normally gravitate towards people who are just like you? Do you fear losing friends and dance to everyone's tune, do you say it like it is, or are you over direct? Have you ever thought whether or not you would choose you as a friend? Take time to make a list of your friend's qualities and your own qualities as a friend.

I love people and am happy to make new friends, but I value and cherish those who have always been there for me and know me almost as well as I know myself. Those who love me for who I am "support knickers" and all, those who believe in me enough and encourage me to run with the most outrageous ideas just because my intuition tells me it could be a winner!

They say friends come into your life for a reason, a season or a lifetime. Do you have some weeding out to do to remove the hard work with little return friends, do you have some thanking to do to the fantastic friends that pick you up when you are down and provide the caring and compassion when you need it most. How does the friendship area in life score right now?

PERSONAL RELATIONSHIPS

An extremely influential person in our lives is the one we invite as our life partner. They say this is a selection we should make carefully as from this one decision comes 90% of our sorrow or our joy! After years of counselling friends and family through life's ups and downs I agree whole-heartedly with this. If we can score our personal relationship highly the chances are that we will have more balance in other areas. Most of us want a special someone to share our life, but what makes it so complicated? Do we look for our life partner being the "be all and end all" in our life? Is it feasible to expect one person to meet all our needs or are we setting our personal relationship up to fail?

What makes a great life partner? We are looking for someone who ticks all the major boxes. Someone who is visually pleasing, superficial as it may seem, the reality is we are usually drawn to attractive looking individuals. We want someone who shares our values, so truth; integrity, honesty, compassion, caring and kind are all high scorers in our life partner charts. And drawing from the singles ads in the newspaper we can not underestimate the all important GSOH! Then there is the ability to laugh at themselves, able to mix in any company, mannerly, respectful and intellectually stimulating. No wonder this is an area that causes much grief and heartache. So have you got it sussed? It may be that we need to throw away the ideals of "perfection" and remember why we to begin with, were attracted to our partner. If nothing comes to mind it may be time to move on!

Is there ever going to be anyone to fill the life partner space? Are we the sort of person who is a partner worth having? Do we give as much as we demand; do we care, share and give as well as being open enough to receive graciously? Are we still keen to have fun and frolics without taking life too seriously? Are we over protective and jealous to the point we sabotage our personal relationship? A very important area to think about as we score this one; do we listen and are we listened to? If we can establish a relationship with that special someone and we value their opinion the major decisions that you make will be fully discussed with your partner and they will be aware of the challenges and the celebrations as they happen, making them your confidante and sounding board. Lots to consider as we rate our relationship, so what's your score then?

HEALTH

For me this is a top personal value; one thing that money can't buy. Most of us are born with perfect bodies and as we travel through life it is about respecting and valuing the gift of perfect health. Our cars can be traded in and upgraded but the bodies we are born with have to last us for the many journeys that we will make over the years. Sure we all over indulge from time to time but it is about respecting and balancing the body to keep in tune. I once trekked in Peru to raise funds for my local hospice in Airdrie, St Andrews. On the long flight over I had the privilege of sitting next to Sister Catherine who was Director at the time. As we chatted about our experience that was about to unfold I revealed that I admired her still being fully involved in the hard work side of fund raising despite being close to retirement age. Sister Catherine looked at me directly with a twinkle in her eye and said in her soft Irish accent "Sure Marion you and I owe it to ourselves to be as fit and healthy as we can, I'm only keeping myself fit and healthy!" I counted climbing 4 times higher than Ben Nevis above and beyond the call of duty for her but she would have none of it because when you work and live with people who are terminally ill it provides the perspective to ensure you cherish the health that you have. Are you cherishing the health that you have or abusing it?

The mind comes into the equation too. This is where we value the power of our own thoughts. Do we feed ourselves positive images of who we are or are we constantly selling ourselves short? Great mental health is every bit as vital as great physical health. The more we love ourselves the better our mental health will be.

Others can have an effect on our mental health however, it is often said that no one can make you feel inferior without your consent, so one of the keys to good mental health is to screen the comments you receive and endorse those that come from people you value and admire. Compliments can be accepted with a simple thank you. You should feel uplifted when others see your skills before your limitations and these are the conversations that we must store in our mental savings account for those emotional rainy days.

Are you making the most of your health? Should you be more disciplined or a little kinder to yourself? Are you due a reward or relaxation to keep you stress free and in the pink? Value your body, respect it and reap the benefits. Now how do you score?

SPIRITUALITY

Our relationship with our soul is the most important of all and all too often under-valued. I class the soul as the very core of whom you are and encourage people to feel that they are good enough as they are. We all have our own type of perfection. I discourage people from comparison ....individuals are unique.

We will always find areas that we fall short in and imperfections can be magnified and blown out of all proportion. Finding out more about yourself takes time and you can't get to know who you are if you fill every waking minute with activity and people.

In the 21st century we have become restless and anxious in our endless quest for purpose and direction. Let's face it, we live in an age where people in the western world have, on the whole, more material possessions and still more on immediate offer by taking out yet another credit card. Possessions don't make us happy long term, deep down we all know this, a sense of purpose does. More and more people are looking for escape routes and paths that take them away from consumerism and greed. The first step to harmony is to get to know yourself fully and that means accepting flaws and the areas that you don't shine as brightly in. Just say "I accept that perfection is a myth and I embrace and love me for who I am." Your strengths and skills and beautiful features make you an individual who is worth getting to know and love.

Lisa my youngest daughter once was delivering a presentation to pupils at a local high school and spoke about loving yourself and being able to say what you are good at. One of the 3rd year girls immediately asked her if that made you "full of yourself!!" Lisa thought for a minute and said "Who else would you want to be full of? If you're not filled to the brim with all that you know you are, then who or what is going to fill you?" How liberating to feel it is enough to be who we are and not hanker after someone else's lifestyle, perfect body or fame and fortune. Love yourself and know yourself fully. Lisa taught these young people a valuable lesson that day; the only person you travel your whole life with is you, be proud to be who you are and enjoy the journey.

Know yourself fully, be happy with who you are and rejoice in the fact we are all different and beautiful in many ways. How well do you know yourself? How spiritually connected are you with, well, you!?

CAREER

How do we view ourselves in the world of work? Women often hold back where men will step forward and present themselves as job ready. What do we have to learn from our men friends then? Research shows that if there are 5 steps to achievement our gender determines how we move from the first to the last step.

Men will start at step 1 , then look at step 2 & step 3 and think I've covered stuff like this before, I'll skip these steps and move onto steps 4 and 5 and hey presto, drum roll please, I've achieved my goal!! They don't go back and check and recheck; in fact often they start at step 3. This shows that in the world of work men are used to taking the risk and pushing on. Sometimes it pays off and sometimes they come unstuck, but either way they are undeterred.

Women on the other hand will start at step 1 after reading and researching all that they can. Then and only then they will move onto step 2, when fully satisfied that they have it right they will progress to step 3. When the first 3 steps are completed they will go back and check that all is in order with step 1 to step 3 and when fully satisfied again, then and only then, will they progress to step 4 and then step 5!! Women on the whole are more cautious about pushing forward without looking at it from all angles. In your career where are you right now? Are you doing what you are capable of or are you holding back? To be all we can be we require to be risk takers. Are you doing what you want to do or what you have limited yourself to?

Only in the late 70's early 80's did women really return to the work place a few months after having their children. Women in charge in business and women who run their own businesses are now on the increase.

The main thing limiting us is our own belief systems. So is it time to look at our careers and manage them with the same confidence that we manage our families and social diaries?

How are you scoring on a scale of 1 to 10 for career satisfaction?

PERSONAL DEVELOPMENT

What do you do right now to grow and develop you to the next stage? This question scares lots of women because they can rhyme off what they do to support others with THEIR personal development but what do they do to develop themselves? Kids are ferried to dance classes, drama groups, music lessons, art class, karate, tai kwan do and many more activities that we hope will help them to grow, develop and reach their full potential. What do women do? Often we forget the buzz and the pleasure, not to mention the confidence boost, which we get from doing something that is just for us and develops our skills in a specific area. The real plus of personal development is that growing and developing in one area gives us the personal boost and belief to move forward in many areas of life.

My own areas of personal development opportunities have been the catalyst for the change that catapulted me into my own business. A fire- walk in The Trossachs the week before Christmas in 2002 (kind invitation from a friend). A trek in Peru in 2004 to raise funds for the local hospice. Raced in the Chinese Dragon Boat Race in 1999. I have read more books on personal development that I can count. It's about choosing to push yourself that little bit harder for that little bit longer till you achieve a goal or a dream and then stop, reflect, review the learning and congratulate yourself for taking the time to invest in you and enjoy all the wonderful memories you've created.

Personal development is many different things to different people. Engaging with a coach is a wonderful starting point for personal development. Booking yourself onto a course of self discovery is another fantastic personal development choice. Buying a book, signing up for a cookery, flower arranging, car mechanics or language class are all ways of moving yourself on as a person and broadening your mind to what is out there that you may love to do or an area that you excel in and there's always these infamous classes with the pole for those of you interested in....vaulting! Take time to take a chance on you for a change and have some fun in the process. What are you doing right now for you?

FINANCE

Dum, dum, dum! What is the bank balance like right now? Do you hide your eyes at the ATM? Are you sitting pretty or is there room for improvement in this section of your Circle of Life? Money is an area that we don't discuss with everyone, and rightly so, but what are our views on it?

Often we say we are not driven by money and money is not what makes the world go round, this is perfectly true. However we shouldn't underestimate the freedom that we get from being financially sound. Earning potential comes down to valuing who we are and what we do. If you do a good job you deserve to be paid for that job, if you work extra hours you deserve to be paid for them too.

If you are raising a family it is about teaching them the value of money and the understanding that in order to get you have to give and earning money can start at any age and stage. Giving money to people we love can bring pleasure, but in our children and young people we have to remember what we aim to teach them, the value linked to cash and the reality in life that we all we work for our pennies and so should they in some small way! A very good friend and coach of mine, Scott MacFarlane, enabled me to have a healthier relationship with money by explaining that money was simply an exchange of energy. We give our energy in the form of the work or service that we provide and the person that receives that service gives money in return as their energy exchange.

Are you over generous with others and then struggle to do what you want to do financially? Take time to have an honest review of what you spend each month and where you spend it and then take time to create the ideal budget for the month.

My father-in-law, Gerry Graham, used to say if you earn £20 and spend £19 you sleep better than if you earn £20 and spend £21!! This is the time for you to review and decide how much money you require, how much you would like to have and how you are going to get it but firstly how are you finances scoring right now?

EDUCATION

This area looks at the academic learning experiences that we have had or would like to have. If we have studied and gained qualifications to do what we do for a living can we become complacent? We are now encouraged to commit to lifelong learning. What learning courses have you completed and what have you done with that learning or what will you do with it? We can learn and learn and never put our learning to use or ever revisit it and realistically this knowledge is of no use to us, it is lost learning.

So do you have knowledge stored away that you want to refresh? Is there a degree of revision required to allow you to use what you know in a positive productive way?

If you have always hankered to do something or work somewhere what is really stopping you? If you are keen to start a new academic learning course research what is out there right now. There are so many flexible learning programmes available that we really have no reasonable excuse not to embark on the quest for knowledge.

If we have not gained the necessary qualifications at school we may not have been ready for the information that was being presented to us at that time but does that mean that we cannot start now? The other thing to think about is the learning style that you have. I talk about VHF learning styles which means people learn predominately through 3 main styles, 'visual' learners who will love taking notes, 'audio' or hearing learners who keenly listen and require no notes and 'kinaesthetic' or feeling learners who want to have hands on approach to learning and get the most from the physical act of doing a task. Find out how you learn best.

Invest some time in looking at learning and rate where you would like to put your time and talents, then just set your vision on the course that you want to start and do it now. There is an old Chinese saying that goes like this "The best time to plant a tree was 20 years ago but.......if you didn't then the best time to plant a tree is now", what does your tree of knowledge look like is it scrawny and bare, full of fruit or are you just deciding what sort of tree to plant! The phrase "the more you learn the more you earn" is used to promote further education showing us that all sections in The Circle of Life are linked and affect each other.

RECREATION

AKA fun! For those of us who remember what that word means! How much fun are you having right now? Have we entered the world of grown up and boring? Have we forgotten how to have fun or is life a laugh a minute? Our leisure and pleasure time can be lost to the world of work or family commitments and we worry that we haven't got everything done at home. The fabulous thing I am about to announce is that fun is a MUST for balance in life; there you have it a legitimate reason to take time out!

We need time to relax with other people, indeed when we are at our most relaxed is when we are at our most creative. What is your idea of recreation? Some people like to wine and dine; others love their sports, others like the great outdoors, books, films or music.

All these pursuits are worthwhile, none are a waste of time so don't feel guilty. As women we need to be reminded that recreation makes us better at the more driven tasks in life by refreshing our souls. I love to walk in beautiful surroundings and climb the bonnie Scottish hills' to escape the hustle and bustle and when I return to my day job I feel enthusiastic, energised and focused more than I was before my time out. Doing what we love to do feeds our soul and awakens our mind.

"Few people do business well who do nothing else" – Lord Chesterfield How freeing and empowering to understand that we need play to keep the balance in our business and in our other areas of life where we are caretaker for our family and friends. When we are children "play time" is the part of the day we value most. When and why does this change?

So with that in mind what would you choose to do with your free time? Don't think you'll get away with saying you have no free time, as that could be an excuse for us all. We need to make time for fun it is never given to us on a plate. What is in your diary that you are looking forward to doing or what have you always wanted to do that may take a little planning?

REFLECTION SECTION

on What do women want

Once you have completed the Circle of Life you can take time to set goals in one or all of your key areas.

- Ask yourself what you want in that area for life success?
- Where are you right now?
- What do you have to do to achieve your goal?
- What will your first step be?
- What will your next steps be?
- How long will it take you to complete?
- When will you start?
- Who will support you on your journey?
- When will you achieve your goal?
- How will it feel when you achieve your goal?
- What will you do to celebrate?
- What will you do next?!!

Treat yourself the way you would your best friend and book the massage, get the walking boots on, dance the night away, take time to browse in the book shop or phone friends and meet for a coffee or glass of wine, the possibilities for time out are limitless and don't need to cost the earth. It is your gift to yourself.

This Circle of Life is a wonderful tool to use on a regular basis and the more often you use it the more comfortable you will become with the visual of where you are right now and the measurement of how far you have to travel to get what you count as your ideal or best outcome.

The Bottom Line - What women want

It is important to continue to goal set and move forward, it's equally important to take time to celebrate your achievements. Often we set and achieve a goal only to find our mood becomes flat once we have reached the destination. Keep moving and shaking! Enjoy the moment, live for today, keep believing and achieving!!

★

NEW BEGINNINGS

This journey that we take together affords us the chance to establish a new and exciting beginning. I, like most Scots, make a big thing of New Year celebrations. We see it as a time to reflect on the last year and prepare to get on track for a spectacular new year where life is lived to the full and all is perfect, moonlight and roses, family harmony, disciplined eating and exercise, less chocolate, less wine, more fruit and veg, gallons of water and we should all be fit as a fiddle before we know it. All well and good and as a coach I spend my working life actively encouraging people to, create the vision, hold the dream, make the effort and think big so why would I have an issue with the New Year Resolution game?

My challenge with it is this; people tend to be so driven to start and by week 2 or 3 of the New Year feel they are total failures if they have strayed off track. Worse still, all goal setting stops until 31st December arrives again.

New Year can be fantastic, symbolic and exciting, a time to plan, to prepare and to focus on the future. However, it's not the only chance we have to do all this and it is not, let's be honest, the best time to make all these plans and promises when realistically our mind and body are in party mode! Why not decide this year to celebrate, party, indulge and reunite with those we love and those we have lost contact with throughout the year and thoroughly enjoy our moment. Let's maximise our moment without thoughts of discipline, denial and tough measures impending. We know we can't overindulge for ever but let's give ourselves permission to enjoy the holiday period with real relaxation and recreation.

'New Year', in its symbolic sense, starts whenever you choose. You can choose the time that you are most receptive to change and challenge and make this your time of new beginnings. Think about what works best for you when you are making plans. Is it quiet time alone to get things straight in your head? Or is it time with your nearest and dearest to chat about whatever it is that really makes your heart sing? Is it time with a coach facilitating a session where your mind is free to wander noting all the ideas and creativity that flows when you are chilled out, knowing that you are being listened to and your thoughts are valued, nothing discounted or dismissed.

It's liberating to decide when your New Year begins and much more fun when the planning of the next stage on life's journey is not in the middle of a party. Give some thought to when you are most likely to put maximum effort into planning and committing to making things happen for you. Have you ever felt that one slip or hiccup meant you couldn't go on? Well good news; everyone experiences these hiccups and slips and the more we face them and address them the better prepared we are for the next step on the journey of life.

No one ever gets it exactly right first time every time, we have to remember that. We all know people who allow the first hurdle to take the feet from them and they never get to stage 2 of their plan. Let's get real here, life is a challenge and if we quit at the first hurdle we can never realise our greatness. Every disappointment strengthens us and prepares us for our next step. It is about seeing disappointment as a chance to pick ourselves up and start again with newly gained knowledge and life experience to stand us in good stead for round 2. New beginnings can be scary but they give us the chance to go where we've never been before and where we never knew we could.

During summer I climbed Ben Aan with my friends Margaret and Jamie and the pleasure I got from Margaret's reaction to the view at the top was almost as wonderful as seeing all three beautiful lochs my self for the first time. Life's not just about our own new beginnings it's also about sharing experiences and encouraging others. The more we begin new adventures the easier it becomes to take the first step out of our comfort zones again and again. It gradually becomes more and more apparent to ourselves and others that we are capable of more than we knew.

Variety, as they say, is the spice of life and whether it is the beginning of a new friendship or a business partnership we never know where a bit of spice will take us! Throw yourself into every new moment with energy and eager anticipation and see the effect it has on creating a full and satisfying future. Danny Wallace's' book "Yes Man" sees him saying yes to all that comes his way, good bad and indeed ugly. Such extremes can be messy and are not required (or encouraged!) Here, I only urge you to make new connections, meetings, clubs, friendships, visions and goals. Embrace life and the opportunities that come your way and then New Year can happen when it suits you best!

REFLECTION SECTION
on New Beginnings

- When do you feel best able to plan your new beginning?

- How do you cope when things don't go according to plan?

- What would make it easier to start again?

- What excites you about new beginnings?

- Who shares your excitement?

- Any new beginnings planned?

- How do you celebrate when a plan comes together?

The Bottom Line - New Beginnings
During a coaching demonstration someone fretted about not completing a goal in the timescale that they had forecast and asked how to deal with the issue. Simple... set a new timescale! We only ever feel pressure and stress when we don't change and adapt. We are human, fallible and imperfect, we stutter, we stammer, at times we fall flat on our face............get over it, smile, laugh, forgive and move on. Choose to begin again and embrace the moment.

★

MAXIMISE YOUR MOMENT

'Life's what happens when you're busy making other plans.'
John Lennon

Where do we begin to maximise our moment? We begin with ourselves. We must invest in freeing our spirit, feeding our soul and totally embracing every moment as if it were our final moment on this earth. No one is promised tomorrow, all we have is now, why waste it? Why give our energy to negative thoughts, challenges that don't concern us, talking about doom and gloom? As we look at making the most of who we are we must be clear about what we don't want and what does not serve us well. By doing this we find our place in the world, our place that provides our respite and harmony with our self. Then we can step into the light and have our moment, live our life in the present tense not constantly looking over our shoulder at what has gone before

There is a Tim McGraw song "Live like you are dying" and I urge you to listen to the lyrics quietly on your own and with your eyes closed, embrace the message. What do you do when you get that kind of news? It is a song written about a dying man who embraces the moment, because the preciousness of time has been brought into sharp focus. Emotionally he loves deeper, speaks sweeter, gives forgiveness that he had been denying, aren't these things we could all be doing? The song covers a relationship between a father and a son and the son reflects that 'all of a sudden goin' fishing wasn't such an imposition'. How many times do we have family events that we brush aside because we are too busy at work or, worse still, we attend and complain throughout about the changes and challenges that had to be made to get there. Maximising our moment means that we shouldn't wait until facing the final curtain to connect with our nearest and dearest, to be the mother, wife, sister, daughter, or friend that we would like to have ourselves, the song sees a man become the man he knew he was but for only the little time he had left. Strange that when time is running out we realise who we are and place great importance on people, exciting experiences and very little, if any on possessions and material wealth. Valuing the people we often take for granted and being there when our friends and family have their magic moments allows us to maximise ours. Let's all live in the moment and do it now! Make today the day that we do the exciting things that set our soul on fire NOW not just one day!

Are we conditioned to steep ourselves in negativity because culturally that's what Brits do? Are we taking the easy road out and joining in with the tittle-tattle and gossip? There will always be a crowd around the storyteller, nosy parker, rumourmonger because they are loud, demanding and if we are honest they are often entertaining but when we walk away are we uplifted, are we challenged are we full of hope for tomorrow? Nope. We're usually left feeling a little uneasy, a little guilty and a little uncomfortable especially if, horror of horrors, we find ourselves smack bang in front of the person we were gossiping about! So first thing to be clear about, gossip does not allow us to maximise our moment, if your nose is in somebody else's business then who is minding yours?

As a coach I am all for planning preparing and having a magnificent vision for the future but that shouldn't detract from the here and now. When I ask people what they want now they struggle. Often their disclaimer for life being out of balance now is that next week, next month, next year, will be so much better. Will it? The best chance we stand in creating a terrific tomorrow is by investing in today. We should programme ourselves to have magnificent moments every day. When I work with children I always ask them what is great about today and they can always give me a list. They live in the moment, excited by the small things, delighted by the people who love them and accepting that life is good now. How much we have to learn from them.

Sometimes when life is good we worry that we are having too much fun. I ask you; can we ever have too much fun? My clients in personal coaching session will come through change and challenge at work where worry and stress consumes them leaving them no free time. We work together balancing the business and striving to make life a priority once again. The most difficult thing for people to accept when they start to live in the moment again and put work in a box at night is that it's ok to have a good time every day. Of course it is! Life is not a dress rehearsal, today is for living and loving as well as working and earning. You work hard, you play hard, simple! Those who disapprove often have not worked out how to make the most of each day and they don't want others to be cheerful and vibrant when they are not. This is not your problem you're only required to make the most of your moment not theirs. Take your place in the world and share your time with those that you want to be with, experience new and exciting events that stretch your mind. When you are fully present you see, hear and feel so much more. Often people do not live in this moment but fret about the next. All this does is give you less appreciation of what you have today. Tomorrow will come any way and when you look back on what should have been a pleasant experience will it be remembered with any clarity or emotion or will it have been a half enjoyed moment as the monkey mind swung from yesterday's news to tomorrow's worry?

I love being with people who maximise their moment and are fully present. They listen to me and engage fully; they ask what's next when I share my vision. They feel they have the time to enjoy the present. They energise me, fill me with enthusiasm and increase my motivation.

People who maximise their moment are positive and optimistic. They are not airy fairy or disconnected from reality. They take the rough with the smooth but they expect smooth. They value people. Money is easier to give than time but it is spent and gone before we know it and, if truth be told, we would rather have more time with our loved ones than more money. Maximising our moment is about allowing ourselves to be time rich again. How will you do that? Spend less, work less, clean less, 'fuss' less? You must decide how you can be time rich again and believe me you can but it requires thought and it requires change Understand what you mean to those who care for you and choose to give of your time not your money. Be confident about who you are, consider your worth and value to those you love and those you work with. Enjoy sharing time with those who are like-minded and those who encourage you. Appreciate yourself and others, listen to different opinions but ultimately make up your own mind about what direction and action you take. All this lets you do what you choose to do now. There really is no time like the present to begin to live life to the max.

Times is very precious and like money it can only be spent once, choose to spend it well and wisely.

Let's look at image to maximise ourselves. Image works on 3 different levels

PERSONAL IMAGE

How you view yourself. Do you see yourself as gorgeous, visually pleasing and worth looking at or are you selling yourself short, focusing on what's missing rather than what's there? I am 5ft 1 inch tall; now I can lament or I can accept. I can tell you how vertically challenged I am or I can tell you I am exactly the same height as Kylie Minogue! Which description leaves the best picture? I am never going to stand out in the crowd because I am head and shoulders above the crowd, unless I'm in a Nursery School! So I will need to stand out in other ways, I am cheerier than most, I dress vibrantly, I don't take myself too seriously and I fully engage with those I meet. I have high self esteem without having delusions of grandeur and I feel good about who I am, give or take the extra _ stone in weight that comes and goes! If you have to ask whether your bum looks big in what you're wearing then choose to wear something that flatters your bum and send the guilty garment to the charity shop!

Our personal image needs to be strong and we need to feel we are enough just as we are. Dropping a few pounds may put us on the track to perfection but while we journey we have to love the skin we are in! My husband Kenny worked beside a guy that always felt he was enough. He used to say 'I wake up in the morning and I canny wait to look in the mirror!' This was said in fun but how good was it for his personal image? When people greeted him with the customary 'How are you?' His response was always "If I was any better it would be ridiculous!" Spreading fun and laughter as well as a positive self image, you can't ask for any better really!

The personal image we hold in our minds and imagination is not always how we actually look. We often sell ourselves short and it is worth seeking out truthful friends, or professional input from an Image Consultant, to discover the colours and styles that make the most of you. The more confident you are the stronger and more positive your Personal Image will be. Getting a match between personal image and projected image means you are congruent and feel good about who you are, warts and all, but it can be a work in progress!

PROJECTED IMAGE

How do the public view you? What sort of projected image do you send out to the world? We create who we are and we decide what we want others to see. Now please don't be thinking I'm a shallow Hal only interested in physical appearance, far from it, but after traveling the earth for fifty(ish!) years I am sure of this; most of us are influenced by the visual image that others project.

We love seeing people who are visually pleasing, often to the degree that we never question whether or not they feel as confident as they look, or if they know as much as they appear to know. We get caught up in the picture that person has produced denoting who they are and we are sucked into believing what they are telling us. Why? Simple! They look the part! How often do we tell our kids not to judge a book by its cover, but in the same breath say always look your best. This is because even if you don't judge a book by its cover there are plenty out there who do!

You never get a second chance to make a first impression. Make the most of who you are by looking and feeling your best. The signal we send out may not be the one that people are receiving because there are some out there who do see past the polished image and pick up the subtle under confident vibe and the self-doubt. We need to feel good about our true self and be as kind to ourselves as we are to others in order to project a whole, truthful, developed, balanced image. It may sound complicated but in simple terms we have to love ourselves enough in order to match our personal image with our projected image. Then we can know ourselves fully and feel happy to be who we are.

People will often have a far more positive picture of us than we have of ourselves. When I work with clients I am persistently telling them to 'fake it till they make it', appear to be confident and competent, appear to take control, and appear to be able to lead the team. It's the old 'duck swimming on calm pond without a ripple and flapping like mad underneath' syndrome. The better we become at projecting the strong positive image the sooner we believe in ourselves and the rest of the world will soon follow suit.

PERCEIVED IMAGE

How do others view you and perceive you? This is a challenging question. To quote our national bard 'Oh wad some pow'r the gift tae gie us, tae see ourselves as others see us.' If we know ourselves fully and are happy with who we are then we are more likely to be perceived in a positive light. We aim to blend at the appropriate moments and shine at the appropriate moments. We want to be comfortable with who we are without making others feel uncomfortable. At the end of the day the old saying, you can please all of the people some of the time but not all of the people all of the time, comes to mind. I aim to be who I am and, to borrow from Buddhist philosophy, I aim at best to benefit others and at least to do no harm. In general people perceive me in a very positive way, however if someone has a different perception of me that is entirely their prerogative. If we want to know what sort of picture is being picked up the only direct way to find out is to ask, listen and decide if you want to endorse that persons opinion. Different people will see different things in you. Some will only notice the clothes you wear or how you have done your hair but others, to pinch a phrase from mega-hit movie 'Avatar', will 'see you', your compassion, your intelligence, your strength and your ability to be who you are.

Ultimately others value you as much as you value yourself. Let's look at our belief systems and measure our

- Self belief
- Self confidence
- Self esteem
- Our self-talk
- Our positive mental attitude, changes from 5 to 15
- What happens to us on our journey to adulthood
- How we value who we are

Today know yourself, maximise your moment, be who you were meant to be

- Know yourself fully or be full of yourself?
- Who else would we want to be full of?
- Stick with those who encourage you, avoid those who limit your beliefs.
- It all starts with your thoughts; make them positive.
- Revisit your success stories more often than your failures.
- Choose a positive image
- Look in the mirror and like what you see

Your history does not define your future but it can be used to your advantage if you sift through your memories and draw strength from the brilliant, vibrant, shining moments by bringing them to the front of your mind. To make the most of now and project that positive image it is vital to reflect on success. On the Soul Sisters Seminars we make sure everyone in the room has their moment of glory, their time to share their success stories from life and work. At this time we ask women to empower others by imparting wee gems of wisdom from their past that have served them well and gifting these experiences to the room to allow others to learn from the magic of the moment. This has proved over and over to be exciting, emotional and extremely worthwhile.

REFLECTION SECTION

on maximising your moment

- What portraits of your success are hanging in your 'Picture Gallery of Personal Pride'?

- What dreams have you shelved because you believe that someone else knew better?

- What dreams do you intend to re-engage with?

The Bottom Line - You are an expert on YOU!
Let's begin our day by stepping into the moment with excitement and eager anticipation about what the day ahead has in store. Understanding that every moment is precious and never comes around again. It doesn't matter who you are, whether you are a mother, daughter, sister or friend, old or young I have never met anyone who could rewind yesterday and start again. Relax, enjoy, smile and most importantly................Maximise your moment!!

★

DESTINATION UNKNOWN

A notion that should fill us all with excitement is that the next page of our book of life is blank and perfectly clean. The script is unwritten, the scene has not been set, and the actors have not been called to the stage to play their parts. Let your imagination run wild and decide what you want; the future is as yet undecided.

Where do you choose to place your energy? When the movie of your life runs from the day that you were born, till the day that you pass, you will have the starring role. You will have directed, produced, cast the supporting roles and written the plot. The best movies take planning and life is no different. Choose to direct your energy towards the most satisfying storyline, one which is unique, uncomplicated and fully connected with people who love and respect you. Begin to understand the power of now, the power of maximising your moment and living in the present with positive belief and a vision that is clear, focused and, above all, true to you.

During the Soul Sisters Seminars hundreds of women have taken the time to enjoy a guided journey of relaxation to 'The Place of New Beginnings', and I know for a fact that it is only when they close their eyes, breathe deeply and start the process of relaxation that the destination begins to slowly take shape and form. They are taking time to plan.

In the final chapters of this, our first book, I ask you to take time to choose where you would like to travel to, who you would like to invite on your journey and when you would like to get there. Exciting destinations are the places that you select to be exciting; they are places where you are comfortable and happy, whether in a new country, new job, new relationship or a return journey to a familiar city, building or career. Your journey may take you to the kitchen table of a good friend to sit with a cup of coffee and a rare chance to deliberate over what has gone before and what is yet to come. No limits, no fear of not belonging, no judging yourself. This is simply an opportunity to step onto the stage in your mind, better known as your imagination, and create. Enjoy the escape from what is and immerse yourself in what could be. It all starts with one wonderful thought of a life lived to the full doing what you choose to do not what you feel you have to do Where you are free to be the person you truly are, full of passion, joy and good grace who is grateful for what they are blessed with and who cares for themselves and others in equal measure. Become someone who expects life to be wonderful, but knows it will not be free of challenges.

We require challenge to test us, to allow a stretch that takes us out of our comfort zone and shows us what we are capable of. We are always capable of more than we imagine. There are untapped talents and skills waiting for the moment you take the dust covers off them and embrace them as yours, you are moving towards fulfilment and balance.

I find this exploration of the mind can often make us weepy and emotional. This is because we come across talents and opportunities that we have boxed up or forgotten. We stumble upon the things that made us truly happy. We are presented with a picture of what we have created and realise it may not be what we want; rather it is what we have allowed others to steer us towards. The big plus in all this is that we can choose now and make the choices bold, bright and exciting but most importantly we can make them our choices, we can decide what we have and what we do. We can, perhaps for the first time, choose to do what makes our heart sing.

Remember your true supporters, they appear from the strangest places and they may not always be your nearest and dearest. We often feel an immediate connection with someone who we meet for the first time but due to our social conditioning are too guarded, private, fearful or even proud to pursue the feeling of the moment. Hold these moments close and allow them to gently unfold into beautiful friendships. We can never have too many friends, we can never tell people we love them often enough. We should embrace those who listen, support and encourage us to be the person we know we could and should be, we need only be brave enough.

Who is there to encourage and champion you on the next adventure? Ask others for help, be it in the form of advice, their talents, their opinions, their life experiences. When you do so you allow them to feel they are valued too.

I have the good fortune of having family that I value, every generation from the wild-child teens to the often too open and honest grannies! My fabulous mother-in-law Thelma Graham was the youngest of seven sisters and four brothers, can you imagine? She has fascinating stories to tell of those who loved and lost and those who never loved at all, of secret loves and celebrated loves, but what she knows better than anyone is that if you can confide in people and ask for encouragement the chances are you will be given it. I believe that people are, at their core, good and while you still have the experiences of the generation before you grab them with both hands. Ask them for their opinions, experiences, guidance and thank them for their open honest advice and encouragement. Never under estimate the pride that they feel in being consulted and included in your life plan and the pleasure that they take in witnessing and being part of your success and achievements. I always feel that my achievements simply must be shared with my mother-in-law and my own wee mammy because they gave what they could to allow me to be who I wanted to be without any grudge, resentment or bitterness and when they were in the prime of their life, these wonderful women now in their 80's certainly would not have had the openings and opportunities that I have been blessed with.

When I delivered my wonderful Soul Sisters Seminar for the first time I asked the ladies in the room to take a journey into the unknown in their imagination. This is a lovely guided journey of relaxation and a chance to plan the next chapter. I asked that in their imagination they invite those who would be interested or knowledgeable enough to help them, to join them in their own private space in their mind where all brilliant and exciting thoughts are born. This brings all sorts of weird and wonderful people back into the moment. Some we know well, some are famous but we have never met, some are with us still and some have passed on. This is a chance to imagine great advisors sharing wisdom freely as we plan the next stage on our journey.

I love the fact that often when I seek counsel in my "Thinking Room" in my head it is frequently my dear old granny Lily Gibson who turns up first in the queue with the spiels and spiels of advice! Lily is often uninvited, as I have an expert in mind that I am about to imagine myself in deep conversation with, when my granny arrives and elbows the expert out of the way!!

My granny, Lily was born and raised in The Gorbals in Glasgow which was a place of community spirit, laughter, love, caring and sharing at the time of her youth. Later years have seen it gain a reputation of being a rough area, represented in books as a place to fear if walking alone at night. Although my own wee mammy always labelled her childhood area as Hutchison Town, never the Gorbals, so she will not be happy with this!

Anyway back to Lily who, by modern day standards, may not have had any great accreditations, labels or successes due to the fact women were destined to be 'homemakers' not 'career girls', her words not mine! But in my book my 'Glasgow Gran' as she was renamed by my daughters, had it all in terms of character, confidence, wisdom and courage. She said it like it was and raised, both my mother and my auntie Lillian, to be happy with who they are. Lily entertained her many sisters and brothers and always said it as she saw it without dancing round the issue or diluting her message. She had her opinion and would deliver it to you clear as a bell, be you male or female, old or young. Can't you see the worth in a woman who knows herself fully no matter what external labels she has had placed on her? And perhaps, more significantly she was a powerful, positive role model despite having none of the titles and triumphs that could have been hers if she had not been born in a later era.

Irrespective of all the learned individuals that I have had the privilege of meeting and working with it is Lily Gibson who, in times of challenge, offers me in my imagination the most precious powerful pieces of advice along with my wonderful, loving dad Bert Gourlay. The difference between them is my dad always presents his advice as an option while old Lil presents hers as the only road! It was not my intention to mention either my granny or my dad here but they arrived in my head with a message that is now in print. Was it my subconscious mind or are they both still somewhere out there? That's a subject for another book, another genre! What I am sure of is the part my ancestors played in my past is worth remembering when I plan my future. They worked hard, lived hard and had a lot less time for play than you or I and far fewer opportunities, but still they can illuminate the way to a better life for us by teaching, even when they are no longer physically present, the lesson that we can be who we choose to be with or without labels. It is the way we conduct ourselves that makes us who we are, not what we are given in way of certificates and diplomas from others.

Absent friends are worth considering when you visit your imagination to plan the next big road trip in life. Who hasn't turned up in your imagination as you plan your next chapter? Who does not come to wave you off or cheer you on? Perhaps family and friends who have been in your life forever have not appeared to motivate you, inspire you and cheer you down this path which has yet to be charted. Are they just too busy, too self absorbed or do they have a touch of the green eyed monster? These may be the people who you don't share your dreams with for fear of sabotage. I give no more thought to them.

I allow my coaches, mentors and encouragers to flood in to cheer me on and I feel the motivation, enthusiasm and drive fill the space in my mind where all adventures begin and all plans are possible. The next goal is set out and moulded and polished and the thought of what is possible inspires me to 'think in ink' once I return from my imagination so that the possibilities are not lost but held on paper to be refined and worked on. Soon the next great dream is being shaped and fashioned. The next destination is in sight and the work begins to make the vision a reality.

Take yourself to this relaxing place of creation often so that you might maintain the passion and recharge your energy. Dream the dream and maximise the moment.

REFLECTION SECTION

Reflection Time Destination Unknown

- Find the quiet spot
- Take the time
- Dream the dream

Bottom Line

The next dream needs time to grow, to be nurtured, to be worked on before it can explode into your life, a dazzle of colour, a blaze of glory and an adventure worth pursuing with all your might. The unknown is an exciting, mysterious new friend.

★

LIFELONG LEARNING

My journey in learning started at Glenlee Primary School where I was happy to learn on the condition that I liked my teacher, if she was a 'shouter' then you wouldn't see me for dust, literally!

I would race home and hide under my bed. The queen shouter was Miss Fergus; I quiver slightly now as I type her name. She had me reduced to tears, 'greetin ma wee heart oot' as my mammy would say. She was close to retirement, seeming ancient to the eight year old me, and the fear she instilled in me blocked my learning and concentration for the year I was in her class. I used to be 'put oot' to school in the morning, I never went willingly, and I would return to the door 3 or 4 times before I made it across the road and down towards the school gate. KNOCK, KNOCK! 'Can I have money for playtime?' KNOCK KNOCK! 'I don't want money for playtime I don't think' KNOCK KNOCK! 'I need a hankie for my pocket' KNOCK KNOCK! 'I don't need this hankie anymore.' This would be called creative avoidance, although I'm sure my poor wee mammy would have had some other words for it. The saying "what doesn't kill you makes you stronger" comes to mind here as this fearful teacher/pupil relationship spurred desire as an adult to research and understand how best to nurture and teach my daughters Carly and Lisa in a way they could enjoy learning and feel knowledge was a gift and not a chore.

Not all my teachers were shouters, one magnificent teacher Miss Morrison saw all that was good in me and prepared me for my secondary education by making me feel I was capable and academically bright. She encouraged me to think about how best to fit in at secondary school. I never felt that I shone academically; I imagined my real skills lay in the way I could get on with and understand people. I must however have been reasonably bright as I passed my 11 plus and qualified for Hamilton Academy the school at that time taking only the top 10% of the students in the area.

Miss Morrison rewarded me with a hockey stick to get me off to a good start as the school had the 'jolly hockey sticks' ethos. I am sad to say that my flirtation with hockey was brief but the effect of that kind act and the encouragement from Miss Morrison remains with me to this day.

Secondary education was a shock to my system and my first impression of the grand old school building was that it was so drab and dull, not a colourful poster or bright learning tool in sight. My teachers wore gowns and delivered their lessons from behind a lectern, learning was not supposed to be fun for goodness sake! Once the shock wore off I settled in and enjoyed most of my secondary education. I grew to love those learning environments where you could relax and converse more freely. The teachers who created environments like these allowed me to make my mark.

My work history was has been colourful, my first full time post being that of a Clerical Officer with The Unemployment Benefit Office. Better known as "The Buroo", or "The Dole", the perfect post for learning how to handle difficult situations and develop an appreciation for the power of humour and fun. My first day on the front counter I was faced with a queue of around 30 people all waiting to make a claim for government benefits. In the 70's there was little privacy and people came up to a high counter and spouted forth their business. Two gentlemen in the queue who were friends and had been paid off from the same company decided to help me out by coming up to the counter together, thinking lots of their circumstances were similar and I could take details from them both at the same time. Wrong! The stress set in and when I asked gent number two what he did for a living he said “well I don’t dae the same work as him ‘cos you’ve put his job title doon as a Labrador...........ah think that’s a type of dug”. Clearly I wanted to write down labourer but had gotten a little confused. We all had a laugh and as the men left and the queue of people waiting to be seen continued to grow, my knights in shining armour paused, faced me and called across the crowded room “ hen it’s been nice meeting you.......the Labrador and me will be back tomorrow to see if you have a giro fur us”

I was employed as a civil servant for 2 years until boredom set in and the clients with a sense of humour set off for pastures new! I decided that the world was my oyster and I set out to see what else was on offer. This led to a year spent touring the West of Scotland with the Blood Transfusion Service, as a Mobile Team Assistant taking blood in every business place imaginable as well as prisons, naval bases, and factories where the benefit of giving blood was an hour off work, then tea and a chocolate biscuit. This job had a variety of roles labelling, beds, stripping, and introductions. There would be several wary glances from commuter on the train as my colleague Janey and I discussed why we preferred being on the beds to stripping! This vampire career choice allowed me to have fun and not have to take myself too seriously.

I spent several years working with high street giant Marks & Spencers’ where I learned the importance of great service and had training that was second to none. I benefited from exposure to management teams that were target driven and standards that were above all others in retail at the time. Most of the staff were female and worked part time. M&S in the 80’s was a pioneer for shift patterns to accommodate families and job sharing for successful balance in business and life.

After M&S I had a 5 year career break and spent invaluable time raising my two gorgeous daughters Carly and Lisa. In between jobs I engaged in lifelong learning and had several business enterprises such as soft furnishings, skin care consultant and educational facilitator. Then the world of work beckoned and like most women

I was eager for yet another new challenge.

I returned to The Job Centre this time in recruitment before taking a secondment which led to a full time post with The Prince's Trust the charity which champions young people who have had limited opportunities in life and provides personal development training and work experience.

I spent seven wonderful, happy and exciting years working in a variety of roles for Prince Charles, eventually becoming Life Coach to The Trust Staff Team in Scotland. This final development led me to set up my own coaching and training company in 2003 and the rest as they say is history.

My business was established and registered in 2002/2003, a dream, a vision, a goal that was brought to reality through hard work and self belief as well as the belief and encouragement of many friends and my colleagues that I worked with in The Prince's Trust. But when I started the dream the destination was very much unknown. I fully appreciate the energy that Susan one of my colleagues from The Trust invested in me in the beginning. It was she who ignited the flame for learning and the belief for success. Phew! So there it is; the path that led to Soul Success Ltd.

★

SOUL SISTERS DIARY

My personal journey towards the launch and premier of Soul Sisters started on Monday 18th June 2007. Business was always quiet during summer and the past year had been a rocky one. I have endeavoured to write my feelings, my true progress, my stumbling blocks and stepping stones of the journey as it was unfolding, otherwise the emotion of the moment is diluted or lost and the growth process is not scribed accurately.

The first 4 years of business had seen profits steadily increase and after the bumper profits made in 2005/2006 I knew the next year would require extra oomph to see the profit graph climb even further. Clearly I had no idea what challenges the universe would sling at me nor did I understand the degree of stamina that would be required to keep afloat never mind to remain positive and creative! This is part of my story and part of my journey. I present it to you in the hope that my experience might speak to you in some way and perhaps inspire, encourage or reassure.

The outward face of Marion Graham is positive, fun loving and very confident but like everyone else I have my shaky moments when I wonder why I didn't choose a path that requires no risk, no creativity and where I don't have to try and market a concept rather than a product to the world. How much easier to sell a bar of soap than a belief system! Especially when, in an often cynical society, people demand proof before they will invest in their own development. Yes I would much rather that there was no requirement for a course or seminar to encourage people to reach their greatness but the truth of the matter ....there is!!

This degree of openness, I must admit is difficult for me because if I am under par, unsure or low in energy, most of the world would never know or ever guess because I choose not to spread misery, instead I retreat and work on refocusing and reenergising. Very few would know what was wrong or how they could help, but those who care always lift me with their words and their concern and I am ready once again to do what I do best, work with people to release their greatness. It may seem strange that someone who encourages others to step into the light has their own darkness and doubt, but no one is, or should claim to be perfect, no one is positivity and joy all the time, but when we dip we rise again. It is not the falling down but the recovery that is important.

The best way to recover is to share your feelings. Choose carefully who you lean on and always ensure that you are willing and open enough to return the favour.

I decided to dedicate 3 months to creating a knowledge of and demand for the Soul Sisters Seminar throughout Scotland. I called on my top 20 women and asked for help, guidance, inspiration and the thing that you need most as a woman in business.... encouragement! I then looked at meeting with women who were influential and in a position of power and introduced the idea of a "Limited Company" single sex seminar. Women everywhere were enthralled, intrigued and keen to know more...... well, the majority were. There were a minority who were too fearful or insecure to think about women empowering other women because they had been conditioned to live, think and work in a man's world. All I can say to the women who were afraid to move on is that the world is ready for women to take their place. I was not suggesting that women alienate men but that they enlighten them about where we are in life and business and what makes us progress and move on. Men are as confused about their place in the world now we have embraced gender merging.

The reason I recount this journey in such detail is to allow other women to understand that there is no such thing as an overnight success. Any thing that is worth having is worth working for and this is written from exact experience as I noted the emotions of the moment as I worked on the development and promotion of the seminar.

MY SOUL SISTERS DIARY

12 Weeks to launch
This was an absolute joy. I began the week with a business coaching session from my own personal coach. I had been working for several weeks on the content of the seminar and all of a sudden it came together. Work and commitments still on going and I had a day in my diary to deliver my final session at a local primary school where I had gifted 6 sessions coaching primary 6 pupils I volunteered as part of a community coaching initiative.
I began to arrange and attend meetings to promote the launch and spoke to women about the content of the programme. I printed handouts and agendas and looked at the questions women would benefit from answering on the day. The course was shaping up well and I was getting a great feeling from it.

11 Weeks to launch
More phone calls and preparation of marketing emails. Meetings with women in education, police force and business development all to establish that the course was on track and meeting the needs of women from these professions.

Next I began gathering names and numbers linked to the media, newspapers and magazines; this was new ground for me so I was cautious about what I said and did, not knowing what was right and what was not. I drafted in help from one of my dear friends Rosaleen Glancy who had just finished her time in paid employment and was beginning a new chapter in life which included just as much work but most of it as a volunteer. Rosaleen was in the running for "Scottish Woman of the Year" in 2004 with women such as

Dame Marie Stubbs. Now you know the quality of support I have! Rosaleen has energy and enthusiasm for all that I do and happily went through the media contacts with me making me feel they were lucky to have the opportunity to meet with me....don't you just need that sometimes!

I attended the book launch of a friend in Glasgow Dr David Hamilton whose second book Destiny vs. Freewill was just about to hit the shops. This reconnected me with my passion to complete my own book. It also gave me the chance to have dinner with some of my women friends from my personal power group and seek feedback from them as to the progress to date. A weekend up north with family to keep me grounded.

10 Weeks to launch

Coaching this week and back to chasing the media again in the hope of an opportunity to spread the exciting story of Soul Sisters to the world or at least Scotland!! My husband had an invite to The Royal Garden Party at Holyrood Palace, Edinburgh and, in my role as a good wife, I was attending too.

Spent time sourcing a venue and getting it right, some were too stark and some over fussy so settled on a newly refurbished traditional local hotel. The venue has a modern look but with traditional service to reflect a day about moving forward into new and exciting territory while valuing the traditions and traits that make us who we are. Opted for cabaret set up with white table cover, lovely coffee and a sit down Sunday lunch, women need to know they are special!

9 Weeks to launch

Another week of meetings and emails as well as lots of interest and enquiries but only 25% of the places booked. Energy drops a little and belief system a little shaky. It can be a lonely job sharing your ideas with the world!

Existing business still to be balanced and new enquiries to existing courses still to be addressed, the world does not stop turning because a new idea has been conceived. Another coaching session with my own coach to keep me on track, 4 weeks into the project this is a must. I must keep on track, focused and believe fully in the new and exciting course that is about to take the world by storm!

Visit to image consultant to ensure that I am presenting my best self and learn more about my image linked to colour projection. I have always prided my self on being well groomed but this was about not just looking good it was about looking wonderful. So, walking what I talk, I invest in myself and in getting the right image for the launch. Weekend in London with lifelong friends Jean and Bobby and the chance to chill and spend money, two of the things Jean and I do best!

8 Weeks to launch

London over and all the more reason to get the right women in the room now, firstly to make the premier a WOW and something that all women will be keen to experience, and secondly to pay all the bills that you accrue after a weekend of the high life!! More coaching clients booked in this week and more exciting women who are moving on so my motivation is high again.

Motivation is high largely due to the 60 minute phone call from my good friend Susan Martin who is a development manager and also one of the best visionaries I know. After speaking to Susan I am wondering why we didn't go straight to booking the Royal Concert Hall in Glasgow!! It just goes to show how rapidly life changes though, because this week we move from low energy to an abundant energy that makes me feel there is no stopping me. This is due to spending time talking to my encouragers, sharing networking contacts and also to passionately playing the premier of Soul Sisters in my head with the degree of feeling and emotion that makes 16th September 2007 the launch of a seminar that changes the way women view themselves forever.

7 Weeks to launch

Off on holiday to Tunisia, spent a lot of time thinking about the success of Soul Sisters and allowed myself to dream about the day the seminar is delivered all over the world! Enjoyed time with my husband to eat, drink and be merry! I'm being wary never to become over serious about my own business. Always allow time to laugh and relax and have fun. When you do this you are still enhancing your opportunities of success by allowing your mind to roam free and become more creative.

6 weeks to Launch
Back from holiday and back to reality. All 2000 of my marketing flyers are printed and ready for distribution. This all seems very real now! The course is fully booked!! A sell out. WOW! what a feeling, excitement and fear all rolled into one. The beginning of the week is spent getting paper work in order, invoicing and chasing booking forms.

Working mid week coaching and delivering training and the end of the week is dedicated to media and marketing. I have an appointment on Thursday with Nick Bevans from The Scotsman; this is the second diary date we have as Nick couldn't make the first one. I have had to push for this and blow my own trumpet, to get the chance to put out there that I am the best coach in Scotland. This came about after my dozen or so emails to various papers and magazines were sent out. I have followed up all with phone calls and second emails but my overall impression is that you need to know someone before they grant you any print space, air time or even acknowledgment of your communication!

My gold dust appointment however is not to be, as a serious family matter takes priority that day. I politely email and ask for a second chance in the hope that Nick won't feel I am playing tit for tat!! I call Lynn Kennedy editor from Up Town magazine as Lynn has agreed to come to the launch of Soul Sisters as a VIP guest and take part in the day as a delegate to allow her to understand the power of personal focus and personal growth. No joy in catching Lynn, the dreaded answering machine kicks in but I brace myself, smile and leave a cheery message reminding her of the wonderful day that she is booked to take part in on 16/9/07. Time will tell if she was serious or just keen to get me off the phone the last time we spoke!

5 Weeks to Launch

As part of the Soul Sisters seminar I have planned a session where we play film footage from real women who have been asked to give their own 60 second stories on life and work success. The challenge now is to round up and film my own soul sisters that I have journeyed with over my lifetime. I plan to have women from every decade from teenagers through to women in their prime who are 80 years young!

My friends now have to be educated more fully on what the seminar is about and what learning we hope will take place. This is not a walk in the park for people who are your life long friends as they are now viewing you in a different role and some adapt to seeing you in your professional role more easily than others. They are not used to taking me this seriously or for me taking myself this seriously but women's development and the success of the seminar is serious business for me.

My friends in business have lived with this seminar since it was an embryo and are more comfortable with what I want from them and at the end of the day we all desire financial success, as well as working in a field that we are passionate and excited about, so the financial profit is a driver too.

So half a dozen of my favourite women fuelled with food and a glass of bubbly and the recording of the 60 second success stories begin! Interestingly enough most people want themselves refilmed but we want real women not polished professional presenters, heart and Soul Sisters stories of what has made them stronger and more focused. My youngest daughter Lisa takes on the role as camera woman and does a great job of putting people at their ease. Lisa has a Masters Degree in Theatre Studies and Scottish Literature from Glasgow University so her education is not going to waste! Even her Auntie Dorothy who is her godmother and a wonderful role model for Lisa is talked into giving us her moments of glory!

I can't thank my Soul Sisters enough for giving of themselves and supporting me in the journey towards the delivery of a seminar that was real, meaning full and entertaining too. More meetings to spread the word booked and attended, and further calls and emails to the media in the hope of establishing interest in the launch.

4 Weeks to Launch

Bit of a non starter this week. Energy dipping and peaking and life continuing along the same lines, could be the weather or just the length of time it takes to market and perfect a dream to make it a reality. I plod rather than fly this week with missed connections and phones that are never answered by real people. I now have to decide when to keep ringing and when to call it a day. Are you seen as persistent when you call every week, and do you stand a chance of a meeting, or do you get labelled a pain in the butt?

I end the week on a high by having a 6 hour girlie lunch with Rosaleen my constant inspiration and champion. We had lunch in a lovely wee Italian restaurant and a couple of gin and tonics later I'm once again selling a unique development opportunity to the wonderful professional working women of the world and I can see the course rolling again and again!

3 Weeks to Launch

Coaching at the beginning of the week and two dates set for stage two and stage three of the filming. Stage two of the filming takes place in Ayrshire mid week and the night is hosted by Carly my oldest daughter who has rounded up half a dozen of her Soul Sisters. Carly is an actor and director and her friends have backgrounds in entertainment and theatre so this should be easy, you would think, but it is amazing how uncomfortable it is for us women to reflect on who we are and embrace and share our story. It seems it is simple to put on the mask of theatre and perform as it is a land of make believe but bearing our soul and linking to our true self takes much more courage and commitment than acting does.

Eventually after a relaxing supper and the compulsory glass of bubbly filming begins. The women were once again magnificent and as Carly was filming this time we had a style that was just a little different too. The main concern was how people's hairdos and outfits would look on camera; yes the professional performers were in preening mode!

This was one of our full on weeks with our third filming day taking place on the Sunday and this was our biggest group yet with 10 Soul Sisters sitting around the table waiting to give us a little of their wisdom. Lisa was back from London on an early morning flight to capture the little gems of information when the girlies arrived around lunch time. This was our most culturally diverse group yet. We had a young American woman Lesley Murphy owner of Curves Fitness Centres, Coral my Australian friend who had been in Scotland for over 30 years now and Lynn my friend from school days who had spent 5 years living in Japan.

The day was a great success; although that same feeling was present when everyone had to reflect on, "what are my achievements", what can I pass on? All these great women over the three filming sessions shared a feeling that they may not be special enough to share their moment. If only they knew that we could have made a feature film on them, not just a 20 minute documentary of some of their wisdom and life lessons.

To close the evening we filmed my own mother who was 82 years young. So the task was complete we had women from 20 something to an octogenarian and there was representation from every decade in between. We had planned to film our teenagers but time had run away with us and we closed the can on what we had!

2 Weeks to go!
Monday our copy of the ladies we had filmed was not playing! Bobby Mackie my friend transfers it to a different format, still no luck. Kenny my lovely husband steps up to the plate and pulls in a few favours and gets it reformatted yet again. We now are running towards the end of the week with no film editing done.

Thursday, Andy Joyce our actor friend takes our Soul Sisters stories from our 20 women and begins to pull together the best bits! After working on it for 2 days we have a 20minute recording of the parts that Andy could save! We lost a lot but he had to go with what we had. Friday is all about getting some balance back with my family and celebrating the 2nd birthday of Josh my gorgeous grandson.

Saturday off to Aberdeen for a family weekend and to relax after all the film challenges.

1 week to launch

All the prepping, printing, getting lists, badges, brochures and final polish is in place. Sound systems checked and staff briefed. Unbelievable, Sunday is blast off!

Blast Off!!

Sunday 16th September 2007 we had women from every imaginable background nervously walking through the doors of The Moorings Hotel in Motherwell wondering what they had let themselves in for. They had given up their Sunday to step into their own power and be who they were meant to be. The day was charged with emotion but the time effort and energy of our research and my support team who comprised of Carly and Lisa my daughters and Jamie McCleary my magic Sound Technician paid off, the seminar was a huge success. On the back of that success Soul Sisters 2 Seminar was delivered again 8 weeks later! Jamie who had worked with the girls programming all the music for each individual session throughout the day was our token man but he blended perfectly, showing that he's definitely in touch with his feminine side!

I felt more nervous kicking this first session off on Sunday 16th September 2007 than I have ever felt before. On reflection I realise the first delivery, which was always going to be precious to me, was a bit like handing your child over to their teacher on the first day of school. You want that person to see all the potential you do and embrace it fully.

The women connected, they laughed and cried and shared their moments of greatness and their moments of challenge. They were all different, they were all special and they all displayed honesty which made the moment magnificent!

ACKNOWLEDGEMENTS

My, oh my, so many magic people to thank and so little space!!

I begin my thank you list with my wonderful, loving family for whom I am eternally grateful. My gorgeous daughters Carly and Lisa who were an amazing source of inspiration at every stage of the journey, as I worked on the book they helped inject the humour and never allowed me to forget that plain English earns you extra points in a world overloaded with jargon. Lisa edited the book and crossed out in red pen the "taking it too seriously" bits as well as many exclamation marks, lots of which I put back in! My lovely husband Kenny who proof read the book and dotted every "i" and crossed every "t" long after my concentration had turned to word blindness. My wee mammy for constantly telling me my daddy would have been so proud if he had been alive, the guilt of not finishing would never have left me so packing in after chapter one was no longer an option!

My fantastic Soul Sisters who have travelled on my life journey with me, Colette in particular who convinced me that short and sweet sells way more books than never ending chapters. My Soul Sisters are friends, colleagues, coaching clients and family, they encouraged me to stay on track when the idea of a gin and tonic sounded way more appealing!

My fabulous men friends Scott MacFarlane and Colin Murray who researched the how's and why's of the publishing world and held my hand through the maze of paper work and technology, and Craig Mackie of The Shine Agency who designed the book but also provided "there, there, there" therapy when I was having my crack up moments!

Finally the magnificent movers, shakers and managers that I have worked with over the years who always made me feel I was smarter than the average coach and trainer. The organisations and decision makers who spent time, energy and cash on training and developing staff by investing in the services of Soul Success Ltd. Thank you one and all, you have made my dream a reality and all that is left to do now is "maximise the moment" and celebrate the joy of reaching the goal. Cheers!

★

ABOUT THE AUTHOR

Marion Graham

Company Director of "Soul Success Ltd"

Marion is one of UK's top coaches and trainers; she graduated in 2002 with a distinction in coaching from The Coaching Academy. ...Europe's leading coaching organisation and worked as Prince Charles's coach for his staff team in Scotland. She is a founder member of The Association for Coaching which is responsible for promoting excellence & ethics in coaching across the UK.

Marion encourages individuals to "maximise their moment" and plan a life journey that is purposeful and exciting where they "balance business" and embrace change and challenge with enthusiasm. Her development sessions are interactive, thought provoking and reflective.

2009 was a year of personal growth and challenge for Marion as she graduated from an International Leadership Programme as well as writing her book "Soul Sisters" which aims to empower women and enlighten men .

Every day is an adventure for Marion and she embraces life to the full, having fire walked, completed the West Highland Way and Moon Walked (for charity in Edinburgh not the planet!), Marion loves life!

For more details on coaching & development training log on to Marion's website on www.soulsuccess.co.uk or visit Marion's Face Book Page and join the Soul Sisters Group, gender specific, for discussions and features.